Business Essentials

Coaching
People

D0806478

If you want to know how...

Train Your Team Yourself
How to design and deliver effective in-house training courses

Appraising Job Performance
How to improve job satisfaction and organisational success

You're in Charge Now!
The first-time manager's survival kit

80/20 Management
Work smarter, not harder, and quadruple your results

Leading Teams
Delivering results through networking

howtobooks

Please send for a free copy of the latest catalogue:

HowTo Books
3 Newtec Place, Magdalen Road
Oxford OX4 1RE, United Kingdom
email: info@howtobooks.co.uk
http://www.howtobooks.co.uk

Coaching
People

'Very readable and well structured' – TRAINING JOURNAL

Develop and motivate your team to achieve great results

Dr Rob Yeung

Revised & Updated 2nd Edition

howtobooks

Published by How To Books Ltd,
3 Newtec Place, Magdalen Road,
Oxford OX4 1RE. United Kingdom.
Tel: (01865) 793806. Fax: (01865) 248780.
email: info@howtobooks.co.uk
http://www.howtobooks.co.uk

First edition 1999
Second edition 2003

British Library Cataloguing in Publication Data.
A catalogue record for this book is available from
the British Library.

Cover design by Baseline Arts Ltd, Oxford
Produced for How To Books by Deer Park Productions
Typeset by PDQ Typesetting, Newcastle-under-Lyme, Staffs.
Printed and bound in Great Britain by Bell & Bain Ltd, Glasgow

NOTE: The material contained in this book is set out in good faith for
general guidance and no liability can be accepted for loss or expense
incurred as a result of relying in particular circumstances on statements
made in the book. Laws and regulations are complex and liable to change,
and readers should check the current position with the relevant authorities
before making personal arrangements.

Contents

Preface

It's a sad fact that few organisations tap the full potential of their people. Most people feel bored and uninspired by their work – the majority of employees would gladly quit their jobs if they could only afford it. This book is aimed at people who want to unlock the potential of the individuals they work with – by coaching colleagues to become more productive and motivated at work.

Work does not have to be a dull and uninspiring chore that people do just to pay the bills. Everyone has unique skills and talents that are waiting to be unleashed – if only someone could help them to find some goal or vision to work towards. And coaching is the key to unlocking that potential to the benefit of the individual, the organisation, and – most importantly – you, the coach.

There are plenty of books out there that will provide complicated models of coaching, but this isn't one of them. Coaching isn't rocket science. It just requires a desire to develop other people and an understanding of a very simple framework that can be as formal or informal as you need it to be. Coaching is as much about making an individual *want* to change as the process of helping then to change itself. This book tells you the essentials – what really matters – if you want to develop other people and at the same time help yourself to deliver results.

I sincerely hope you find this book useful. Good luck – and let me know how it goes!

Dr Rob Yeung
Kiddy and Partners
E-mail: robyeung@robyeung.freeserve.co.uk

1 · Understanding Coaching

'Understanding what coaching is and why it's important is your first step to becoming a great coach.'

In this Chapter:

1 BENEFITS OF COACHING

2 LEARNING TO PULL, NOT PUSH

3 COACHING ATTRIBUTES AND QUALITIES

4 A FIVE-STAGE MODEL OF COACHING

Do you want to work in a place where people enthusiastically face new challenges and learn new skills? Would you like to work with colleagues who set high standards and seek to surpass them? Of course you would.

Coaching is about unlocking the potential of your colleagues to maximise their effectiveness at work. But it's about helping, rather than forcing, people to learn and develop themselves. It is as much about giving them the motivation to develop themselves as it is about giving them the ability to change.

Some people call this process coaching; others call it mentoring. But let's not get caught up in unnecessary jargon – what is important is that we are trying to help others to develop.

Coaching is challenging for both you the coach and the person being coached – but anyone can learn it, especially if you take it one step at a time.

Coaching involves investing time and energy in others to reap a more productive, effective and contented team of people around you.

IS THIS YOU?

■ I know coaching will help the people that I coach, but what's in it for me?

- ■ We spend a fortune paying for people to go on training courses and never seem to see any benefit.

- ■ People around here spend so much time watching the clock – they don't seem to care about their jobs. I wish I could find some way to motivate them.

- ■ I'd like to coach but I'm worried that other colleagues will think I'm just wasting my time.

- ■ Frankly, I know that my team could be working more pro-ductively.

1. BENEFITS OF COACHING

It's a common misconception to think that coaching is something you do only to help other people out. There are benefits for yourself as well as the organisation where you work. In fact it would be foolish **not** to do it.

Most importantly, **coaching others benefits you**. Through coaching, you will improve the skills and capacity of those around you to take on more work, which will in turn make your job easier. In addition, you will:

■ Be recognised by others as having the ability to develop others, which is increasingly a key skill that is required of top managers.

■ Have the satisfaction of seeing others grow and get better at their jobs.

■ Hone your own interpersonal skills – many of which can be applied to all human relationships, in and out of work.

■ Create a strong following – after all, if you help other people, they are more likely to help you out.

For the person you are going to coach or the **coachee**, he or she will:

■ Have an opportunity to work towards their career goals.

■ Get feedback on their strengths and weaknesses and be able to speak in confidence about problems or issues.

■ Be able to discuss new ideas and acquire new skills.

Your organisation should encourage you to coach others, because it will:

■ Gain a more motivated and productive workforce.

■ Retain its employees by creating a culture that encourages people to learn new skills rather than stagnate and get bored.

■ Improve the quality of the work done by its employees.

> *Do coaching because it will help the people around you. But do coaching most of all because it will help you.*

2. LEARNING TO PULL, NOT PUSH

Surprisingly, a lot of managers and supervisors still think that 'managing people' means telling other people what to do. They assume that employees – like mindless animals – will only do their work if they are only given explicit instructions and pushed or goaded to do as they are instructed.

However, the adage goes that if you treat people like animals, they will behave like animals. Making decisions on behalf of others and delegating work to them in a top-down fashion is a sure-fire way to demotivate them. Increasingly, the people who are the best at managing others are those that spend time coaching others – or 'pulling' them towards a common goal by establishing their motivations and interests, and involving them in making decisions about the kind of work that they should be doing.

Coaching is about providing encouragement (e.g. 'Come on, you can do it!') as opposed to threats (e.g. 'Do it or else!'). It's about involving and exciting – or even inspiring – people rather than directing and controlling them. And it's about getting people to want something, not telling people what you want.

> *Coaching is a method for guiding and supporting, not directing or instructing, individuals in their pursuit of improved performance at work.*

Coaching can involve giving feedback on performance, challenging occasionally, and providing emotional support too. But the essence of coaching involves asking questions rather than issuing instructions.

3. COACHING ATTRIBUTES AND QUALITIES

Later chapters cover some of the skills that a good coach needs. However, there are some key attributes and qualities that a good coach should have:

- **A belief in coaching.** If you are only paying lip service to coaching or give the impression that coaching isn't very important, your coachees will probably not treat it very seriously either.

- **Respect for the values of other people.** Just because you may want to succeed in your career and have more responsibility doesn't mean that everyone else does too. People differ in what they value in life and you will just have to accept these differences.

- **Patience.** Different people learn at different rates, and some people may take longer to understand things. It may be frustrating at times when others cannot identify solutions as quickly as you can, but being impatient and hurrying a coachee will only undermine their confidence.

■ **Good judgement at all times.** This book gives you a framework for coaching rather than a rigid process that must be followed to the letter. It is aimed at helping you to think about some of the steps that may be involved as well as some of the challenges or difficulties that you may encounter. However, no single book can tell you everything you need to know about coaching. If your common sense tells you that a slightly different approach might work for one of your coachees, then try it out.

> *Common sense is an uncommon quality. If one coaching approach does not work, then try something else.*

4. A FIVE-STAGE MODEL OF COACHING

Coaching involves a series of five broad steps. A lot of coaches follow these stages — even if they don't actually realise it. The five stages are:

1. Setting up.
2. Building rapport.
3. Assessing the situation.
4. Providing feedback.
5. Making changes.

During the first step, you need to figure out who to coach and how you are going to approach them. The second stage involves building a trusting relationship to enable a coachee to feel comfortable speaking candidly. The third stage is then about establishing their career goals and aspirations. The fourth stage involves presenting objective feedback on a coachee's current performance to them. And the final step – which is typically the lengthiest – requires working with a coachee to commit them to making changes in how they behave in order to help them achieve their career goals, while hopefully also making them a more productive member of the team.

IN SUMMARY

Understand that one of the biggest beneficiaries of coaching is yourself – it doesn't just benefit a coachee. However:

■ Recognise that coaching is very different to how you may have been (or are currently) managed or supervised. It's about generating enthusiasm and willingness rather than telling someone what you think they should be doing.

■ Realise that coaching isn't easy. You have to be patient and demonstrate respect for the choices that your coachee makes. But above all, you must really want to help develop other people.

■ Use the five-stage model of coaching as a framework for you to think about coaching in a systematic way. Thinking and preparing for each step will help you to deliver the best results.

2 · Setting Up

'Preparation and forethought are the keys to initiating a successful coaching relationship.'

In this Chapter:

1 CHOOSING WHO TO COACH

2 INITIATING CONTACT

3 AGREEING PARAMETERS

4 SETTING GROUND RULES

No one has as much time as they would like to have. And coaching takes more time than most people think. So you need to think carefully about who to coach first.

Not everyone will be familiar with being coached. Some people may even be downright suspicious of it, so it is up to you to sell the concept of coaching to your prospective coachees.

However, coaching is not about achieving overnight success. Although the details of how, when and where to coach may seem trivial, a good coach will pay attention to these and explain the nature of the coaching relationship so that both you and the coachee get the most out of it.

> *If you don't sell the coaching relationship well enough, you could be wasting your time completely.*

IS THIS YOU?

■ I want to coach my team but don't know where to start.

■ I point out the mistakes in other people's work, but they don't seem to learn from the advice that I give them.

■ The people around me all seem to have different issues. Who should I coach first?

■ I have too much to do to coach everyone all of the time. How can I structure my time most effectively?

■ I have tried to coach people in the past but was disappointed with the limited results.

1. CHOOSING WHO TO COACH

Before approaching a prospective coachee, try to spend a little time thinking about the issues that are likely to come up when you coach any particular individual. Different types of people can each require a very different approach.

In very broad terms, most coachees fall into one of four broad categories:

■ **Remedial coachees**. These people may be struggling with their work – perhaps because of a lack of interest or motivation. Maybe they have personal issues that are affecting their work performance. Or it could be that they lack the skills or knowledge to do their jobs effectively. Your role as coach with these people would be to provide the support that they need to catch up with their peers.

■ **Day-to-day coachees**. These people may be performing competently in their current jobs, but you know that they could be achieving more. Perhaps you see occasional flashes of excellence in their work but for the most part observe that they don't put as much effort into it as they could. Your role as coach would be to work with them to identify tasks or projects that would inspire them to inject more effort and time into their work and therefore achieve more.

■ **Coachees undergoing change**. Some of the people you work with may be doing quite well in their current role. But their performance could easily take a turn for the worse when their circumstances change – for example if they find themselves being given a new role or changed priorities and working conditions. Or perhaps their workload has increased dramatically. Change can be unsettling for people – presenting you with the opportunity to help them maintain a high level of effectiveness in their work during the process of change.

■ **High-potential coachees**. These individuals usually stand out from the crowd. They are intelligent, driven to succeed and willing to invest considerable hard work in their careers – volunteering for projects and staying late to meet challenging deadlines. They may also be younger than other members of the team. And they make no secret of their ambition to climb the organisational hierarchy and take on more responsibility. However, many high-potential individuals focus too much on their future aspirations and may be overestimating their current abilities. So your role would be to help them think about how to not only meet the expectations of their current roles but also put together a plan to meet their longer-term career needs.

So ask yourself who you want to coach and why. Is it to raise substandard performance up to acceptable levels? Or is it to groom the next generation of leaders within the organisation?

Be clear in your own mind why you want to coach any individual. But also be open-minded and ready to revise your opinions if you discover that you are wrong.

Peer coaching

Most people think of coaching as an activity that managers do to their teams. Or it might be something that an external consultant (and I admit to falling into this latter category as a business psychologist) may do with a manager or other individual.

However, there is growing interest in 'peer coaching' – i.e. providing mutual coaching support to a colleague who is the same level as yourself. There can be unique benefits to this form of coaching, as you can use a colleague as a sounding board for the sorts of issues that you face – as well as being able to practise your coaching skills on a colleague in a safe environment. Might this work for you?

2. INITIATING CONTACT

Once you have decided who might be a likely candidate for coaching, you will need to set up a meeting to discuss how the coaching relationship could work. Choose somewhere quiet to have the discussion.

The following points may help you structure the agenda for the pre-coaching meeting:

- Explain why you think that the individual could benefit from coaching.

- Ask the coachee whether he or she agrees that coaching is the right thing to do.

- Agree when, where and for how long you should have sessions.

- Discuss what ground rules will govern the coaching relation-ship.

All of these bullet points are covered in the rest of this chapter.

Selling the benefits of coaching

A critical step is to get a potential coachee's acceptance or buy-in to the idea of being coached. Of course, if you are an employee's manager, a potential coachee may feel that he or she has no real choice but to accept. But, as we all know, there is a big difference between wanting to do something and being made to do it.

Consequently, you need to persuade the individual by 'selling' the idea of coaching. Spend some time before the meeting thinking about the arguments that you will present to your coachee. You may want to refer back to the benefits that were outlined in Chapter 1. But remember that this is about persuasion rather than coercion – about enthusing the coachee rather than pressurising them into a coaching relationship.

Answering questions about coaching

Your coachee may have questions about your reasons for coaching them as well as the coaching process itself. The following are not uncommon questions:

- Why are you singling me out for coaching?

- Why not send me on a training programme instead?

- Why do you suddenly want to coach me when you've been telling me what to do for months/years?

- What if I say that I don't want to be coached?

- Do you think I have a problem that needs sorting out then?

There are no scripted answers for how you should respond to these questions. However, be prepared to give responses that make sense to each and every person that you may want to coach. How would **you** answer any questions that they may have?

> *It may take days, weeks or even months for a person to come round to the idea of being coached. But this is one step that cannot be forced.*

3. AGREEING PARAMETERS

A single coaching session will have little or no effect on improving a person's skills and changing their behaviour. After all, would you expect to be able to play the piano after only one lesson? Playing well requires hours and hours of practice, as well as advice and ongoing support from a good teacher. So make it clear to the coachee that you would like to set up a series of coaching sessions.

However, there are also other parameters that you need to consider. Setting a coachee's expectations beforehand will lead to a more fruitful coaching relationship. So think about the following issues:

■ **Frequency of coaching sessions.** It is a good idea to have a break of at least a week between sessions, but some coaches and coachees only meet once a month or less. The nature of the issue may help you to decide the frequency of sessions. Think back to the four categories of coachees. A high-potential coachee might only require a session every few months to put together a plan and ensure that they stay on track for achieving the long-term goals that you have together identified. On the other hand, a remedial coachee with a specific issue or problem could require weekly coaching sessions until the issue is resolved.

■ **Duration of each session.** Again, it depends on the nature of the issues that the coachee may be facing. For example, if you are meeting to give a coachee tough feedback about their underperformance, you may need several hours to have a meaningful discussion with them. On the other hand, if you are meeting weekly to discuss a problem that a coachee seems to be handling well, then perhaps half an hour may be sufficient.

■ **Time and location of sessions.** In most cases, the time does not matter and the location will probably be your office or whatever meeting room happens to be available. However, you may sometimes want to be away from the office – for example if someone needs coaching on a very sensitive issue or if it is the only way to meet without being interrupted by colleagues or customers. Or maybe you want to put a nervous coachee at ease by choosing a less formal setting – for instance over coffee or lunch.

Coaching requires sustained effort, practice and guidance over a period of time. There are no quick solutions.

Practical tips for good coaching

The following pointers may also help you to structure a successful coaching relationship:

- **Book the coaching sessions in.** Once you have decided how often you should have coaching sessions, schedule them into both your diaries immediately. Try not to let non-essential meetings or other pieces of work take precedence.

■ **Put time aside to plan your coaching sessions.**
Coaching isn't something that you can do without some
preparation to review your notes from the previous session
and think about how you want to structure your next
session to ensure that you use the limited time to best
effect. What issues might the coachee raise? What questions
might you want to ask?

■ **But be flexible.** For instance, if either you or the coachee
has had a bad day or has a deadline to meet, you both need to
have the option of postponing until a later date. Just don't let
this happen too often. And make sure that you apologise for
doing so and explain why you need to postpone.

4. SETTING GROUND RULES

At the beginning of a coaching relationship, you need to set
ground rules for how you will deal with each other and how
you will treat the information that the coachee tells you.

There are two particularly important ground rules that you
may want to discuss.

Confidentiality

Confidentiality encourages a coachee to be more open with you. After all, would you feel comfortable talking honestly, for example, about the mistakes you have made if you knew that the other person was then going to tell all of your colleagues?

You therefore need to assure your coachee that you will not talk about the content of your discussions with anyone else. Even if you may think that telling someone else could help your coachee, think carefully about it. And, wherever possible, ask your coachee for permission before doing so – for example, 'I'd like to tell the HR manager about the person who is harassing you, but I need your go-ahead first.'

Of course, if a coachee confesses to a major mistake or wrongdoing, you may be forced to break confidentiality to deal with it – perhaps by reporting it to someone else to set matters right.

Boundaries

It can also be useful to set boundaries around what you will or will not discuss. For example, some coaches do not feel comfortable talking about personal issues such as relationships with a spouse. If you are not comfortable about discussing such matters, make it clear to your coachee.

After all, coaching differs from counselling. Coaching is aimed at developing the personal and interpersonal skills of a coachee so that he or she can work more effectively, efficiently and enjoyably in the workplace. Counselling often touches on personal issues such as relationships at home, traumas, childhood experiences and other sources of unhappiness that coaches are not qualified to discuss. An unqualified counsellor can actually make a person unhappier, so avoid offering advice on topics you are not qualified to discuss.

IN SUMMARY

The first step of the five-stage model requires you to plan before you initiate contact. Selecting coachees requires some forethought and planning. Ask yourself who you want to coach and why. Once you have decided, remember to:

- Sell the idea of coaching to potential coachees as coaching is a waste of time if people are only paying lip service to it.

- Book in sessions and set time aside to plan and prepare for each session.

- Discuss issues such as confidentiality and boundaries with your coachee.

3 · Building Rapport

'Having an honest and open dialogue can't happen until the coachee trusts that you have their best interests at heart.'

In this Chapter:

Right now, would you feel comfortable speaking to your boss and admitting all of your mistakes and failings and the mistakes from the past? Of course not – yet coaching requires a coachee to be completely open with you. In order to achieve that level of honesty, you need to invest effort in building a rapport with your coachee. And a rapport is not something that you can force – it is something that happens when a coachee feels valued and respected.

However, you can speed the process of rapport building by using key interpersonal skills. Specifically, you need to learn to ask a variety of questions, listen to what is being said and respond appropriately – in a way that will gain the trust of a coachee. Only then will you be able to coach effectively.

However, building rapport is not a step that is simply completed in order to move on. You need to build rapport at the start to get the coaching relationship off the ground, but also consciously maintain the rapport for as long as the coaching relationship exists.

IS THIS YOU?

- How can I get coachees to start talking about their aspirations and the issues that they face in their work?

- I don't think that my coachee trusts me enough to be completely honest with me.

■ My coachee and I seem to be spending a lot of time talking about fairly superficial issues – I find it difficult to find out what's really important to her.

■ What techniques can I use to put a coachee at ease?

■ I'm not sure about the extent to which I should be talking about myself either.

1. ASKING GOOD QUESTIONS

Coaching is much more about asking questions than it is about talking. Rather than providing your coachees with all of the answers, the aim is to ask questions that will make them think for themselves.

As you coach someone, you will need to ask questions to prompt coachees to articulate their personal and professional goals. Further questions will help to establish their current skills and abilities. And yet more questions will help them to identify potential courses of action and plan for achieving their goals.

Open questions

In general, coaching involves the use of open questions – i.e. questions that do not force coachees into either a 'yes' or 'no' response. Open questions encourage a coachee to talk. In fact, you won't go far wrong if you can start a relevant question with one of the following:

- 'What?'
- 'When?'
- 'Where?'
- 'Why?'
- 'How?'
- 'Who?'

Questioning, not commenting

Learn to ask questions rather than make comments. It is natural, for example, that you may want to remark on what a coachee tells you. You might agree or disagree with their point of view, or you may think that you have a solution to their problem. However, resist the urge to share your thoughts with your coachee.

In your role as coach, it would almost certainly be more appropriate to ask further questions to encourage more discussion. For example:

- 'Tell me more about. . .'
- 'What impact did that have on. . .?'
- 'Why do you think it happened that way. . .?'
- 'It's interesting that you feel that way. Why is that. . .?'
- 'Why did you choose to. . .?'

And so on.

> *Use questions to draw insights from your coachees. Your challenge is to help them learn to think for themselves rather than rely on you for the answers.*

Tapping into feelings and emotions

Many people are wary of talking about their feelings. But in order to coach someone effectively, you need to understand every aspect of that person. You need not only the facts but also the feelings and emotions that go with those facts. What makes a coachee tick? This is especially important in the early stage of building rapport.

Try to cover the following areas to learn more about your coachee as a person:

■ What do they like about their work? What projects have they worked on that they really enjoyed and why?

■ What do they most dislike about their work? What most irritates or frustrates them about the organisation, their colleagues or the work itself?

■ How does this job compare with other jobs they may have had?

■ How does he or she feel when things don't go well?

■ What would they like to get out of their work in the coming months or years?

■ How does the job fit with their personal aspirations?

Asking questions that elicit emotions and feelings will help you to find out what is important to a coachee and the best way to motivate them to change. However, a coachee could be suspicious if you have not asked these sorts of questions in the past. So take it slowly – you want the coachee to feel that you are interested in them on a personal level. You do not want them to feel that they are being interrogated!

2. LISTENING

Listening to what your coachee has to say demonstrates that you are interested. It encourages a coachee to open up and tell you more about themselves and their performance at work. Listening helps to build a coachee's confidence that it is acceptable for them to talk candidly.

As a rule of thumb, a coach should be spending less than a third of the time talking. For the other two-thirds of the time, you should be listening and giving your coachee time to think.

Listening is not the same as just hearing something though. Hearing is a passive process, while listening is an active process, a skill that you have to work at.

> *Failing to listen can lead to misunderstandings and confusion, or even bruised feelings and embarrassment.*

But we can all think of meetings we have been in when we have been pretending to be involved and interested but only listening in a very superficial fashion. You can listen out for key words while allowing your mind to wander. But in order to coach effectively, you need to pick up not only the facts that a coachee is telling you, but also on any unspoken feelings and emotions. For example, if someone says one thing but their face or voice is telling a different story, it's up to you to explore what is really going on. As a coach, listening only to the facts is just not good enough.

Then try to recognise the emotions that may be involved:

- 'I can tell that you're feeling frustrated by. . .'
- 'You must be so happy that. . .'
- 'I know that you must feel disappointed that. . .'

3. ACTIVE LISTENING

Non-verbal cues or 'body language' play an important part in showing that you are listening. You don't want to undermine the coaching process by giving a coachee the impression that you are disinterested or have 'heard it all before'.

Think about the last time you tried to have a conversation with someone who didn't seem interested. How did it make you feel?

Consider the following to show that you are interested:

- **Take notes.** Not only will this help you to keep track of your coachee's issues (which becomes particularly important when you may be coaching several people over a period of many months), but it demonstrates visibly that you are attending to what is being said.

- **Use your body.** Leaning towards someone during a conversation sends the message that you are interested in what they are saying. Occasional nods of the head and eye contact also encourage further dialogue.

■ **Observe and mirror facial expressions.** People naturally tend to mirror the facial expressions of those around them – hence the adages that laughter and yawning are contagious – which again demonstrates that you are listening.

■ **Make affirmatory noises.** Good conversationalists use words and phrases such as 'uh-um', 'go on', and 'yes' occasionally to show that they are following what is being discussed.

Most people use non-verbal cues in a fairly natural way but only a very small minority of people use all of these cues all of the time. And if you are new to coaching, you may have plenty to think about in terms of what the coachee is saying and the questions that you are going to ask. So make sure that you do not neglect your non-verbal cues.

Summarising and reflecting

An additional method to show that you are listening is to paraphrase what is being said. But this also helps you to ensure that you have understood everything correctly. You might, for instance, begin a sentence with:

- 'From what I'm hearing, you seem to be saying that. . .'
- 'It sounds like. . .'
- 'Let me see if I understand you correctly, you said that you. . .'

4. DEMONSTRATING EMPATHY

It can be easy to seem dismissive of other people's problems. For example, if you have been using a particular computer system for many years, you may have forgotten how difficult it was when you were learning to use it for the first time. Earlier we discussed the importance of recognising a coachee's feelings. Consider this the next step. Showing a coachee that you not only recognise how they feel but can identify with it is a great way of building rapport – it shows that you are not just a colleague but also a person with anxieties, hopes and feelings too.

Lack of empathy could make you appear patronising or unsympathetic, which would discourage the coachee from continuing to be honest with you. Try putting yourself in the shoes of your coachee. Whether a coachee is telling you about happy circumstances or a difficult situation, try to imagine what it must have felt like and respond accordingly.

> **Empathy is a vital trait for encouraging a coachee to trust you.**

Coaching is not judging

Whatever mistakes a coachee reveals to you, you must resist judging them. People naturally fear being put down or feeling that they are being judged. So make sure that you don't criticise, leap to conclusions or dismiss them out of hand.

If you respond impatiently or put someone down unintentionally, make sure that you find an appropriate moment to apologise sincerely. Saying 'I'm sorry' or 'I was wrong' and meaning it will do a lot to repair any breakdown in communication.

5. RESPECTING THE CHOICES OF OTHERS

You may be tempted to tell a coachee what they should be doing. It can be frustrating when you can clearly see a solution that is far from obvious for a coachee. Or perhaps they arrive at a different solution despite having the same facts as you. However, this illustrates a key difference between teaching and coaching.

Teaching is a process by which an 'expert' shares information with a student. The teacher is assumed to know what the 'right answers' are — which is usually true when the student may be sitting an exam of some sort. In situations outside of the classroom, however, there are rarely 'right' or 'wrong' answers.

Similarly with coaching — matters are rarely black or white. It is more likely that there are a variety of solutions to every problem. For example, consider a hypothetical situation in which a customer has written a letter of complaint to your organisation. One person might respond by phoning the customer immediately, while another might respond by writing a letter back to the customer. A third person might want to consult other colleagues about the best way to tackle the situation.

In very few instances is it possible to state categorically that one solution will definitely be better than another. And therefore you need to allow a coachee to come up with their own solutions.

Use discussion with a coachee to generate ideas, options, and opportunities that would work for them.

6. DISCLOSING

A good method of building rapport is to disclose – or share something about your own life with the coachee. Disclosure is about admitting that you have limitations and make mistakes like any other person. By disclosing, you are implicitly making it acceptable for your coachee to admit their problems too.

There are different ways of disclosing, for example:

- **The humorous anecdote** – revealing some mistake that you once made in a funny story. This often helps to lighten the atmosphere.

- **The learning anecdote** – a story where you begin by describing a mistake you once made and then use the story to illustrate the lesson that you learned from it.

■ **The personal anecdote** – a situation where you talk about your personal hopes, fears, limitations and so on, with the aim of boosting your coachee's confidence.

Disclosure, like empathy, shows that you are not an infallible person sitting in judgement of your coachee, but merely a human being with their best interests at heart.

IN SUMMARY

Rapport, the second step of the five-stage model, is an essential part of the coaching process. Without it, you will never be able to delve beneath the surface of what the coachee is saying. The keys to building a strong rapport are to:

- Ask a broad range of questions to get a coachee to talk about their needs, hopes and fears, and ultimately to generate solutions to the challenges that they face.

- Use your body language and techniques such as summarising and reflecting to show that you are listening.

- Remember that talking honestly about difficult situations, mistakes and feelings is not easy, so make sure that you show that you appreciate and understand your coachee's feelings and points of view.

- Reveal some of your own personal faults or tell a coachee about some of the mistakes you have made in the past.

But rapport cannot be forced. So take your time to let it develop.

4 · Assessing the Situation

'Help a coachee to set a goal then establish what he or she is capable of achieving.'

In this Chapter:

People differ in what they want to achieve at work. One person might have his fingers crossed about getting a promotion while another might want to become sales representative of the year. Yet another might aspire to become the youngest chief executive in the history of the company. Someone else may want interesting and varied work, but not at the cost of their personal life.

A major challenge for you then is to help your coachee to identify a realistic goal, career objective or vision. But developing a long-term goal is the relatively easy bit – anyone can come up with a dream of being successful. The more difficult task is to assess what your coachee is capable of at the moment in order to decide how to help them achieve their objective.

IS THIS YOU?

■ I've established a strong rapport but now need to focus on helping my coachee to think about their performance and impact on others at work.

■ This coachee doesn't want a career – just a job – so how can I motivate him?

■ I think that my coachee is deluding herself about her performance at work.

■ I'm frustrated because my coachee has more than enough ability but lacks the confidence to do more.

■ How can I help my coachee to identify a career goal that will truly motivate them to do better things?

1. LEARNING TO CHALLENGE

So far we have established that questions are necessary to gather information about a coachee's aspirations, likes and dislikes about their work. But it is often also necessary to use questions to challenge what a coachee is saying. What they say should not always be accepted at face value.

Consider a hypothetical situation in which a coachee says, 'Everyone in the team really appreciates my work.' If you have reason to believe otherwise, one approach could be to dispute the coachee's belief with a statement such as, 'Actually, both Peter and Nita have complained about your quality of work in recent weeks.' But the statement could easily come as a shock or surprise to a coachee and make them feel defensive.

A more subtle – and more successful – approach might be to ask the coachee to talk about their relationship with each person on the team individually. Perhaps you could then ask further questions about how those individual team members might rate the coachee's work quality.

In this way, you can help coachees to uncover and accept the truth about themselves, so they gradually learn to think about their quality of work, relationships with colleagues and customers, and so on.

> *Don't be afraid to challenge what is being said. However, do it by asking a question rather than making a statement in the first instance.*

Spotting generalisations

You can identify negative generalisations – in which coachees say something about themselves or others that is either misconceived or simply wrong – by phrases such as:

- 'I've never been any good at. . .'
- 'I can't. . .'

- 'They always say that. . .'
- 'People never give me a chance.'

Positive generalisations are much easier to spot. For example, coachees may overestimate their achievements or assume that they have better working relationships with other people than you know is true. So be ready to challenge a coachee when they think too highly of themselves as well.

Challenging with finesse

Furthermore, don't confuse challenging with putting someone down! Remember to demonstrate empathy whenever you challenge. It might help to preface your challenge with a statement such as 'I can understand that you might feel that way, but' and then to use a question such as:

- 'Is that always true?'
- 'Why do you believe that?'
- 'Why can't you? What would happen if you could?'
- 'Can you not think of a single occasion when you might be able to?'

However, even the most insightful of questions may sometimes fail to have the desired effect. Perhaps you have tried every question you can think of to challenge a coachee's misconceptions or false beliefs. Only when you have made every reasonable effort to challenge through questions should you allow yourself to say what is really on your mind.

2. UNDERSTANDING THE IMPORTANCE OF GOALS

Few people have a clear idea of where they want to be or what they want to be doing in the future. And it is difficult for most people to think far into the future because things always crop up – such as unexpectedly having a family, being offered a better job elsewhere or being made redundant. Who can anticipate such things?

However, there is still value in helping a coachee to think about where he or she would like to be in the medium term. For most people, planning for six months to a year in the future is not unreasonable. For the high-potential coachees that we mentioned in Chapter 2, you may want them to think about planning for much longer time horizons of perhaps three to five years.

> *'The people who will win are those with a clear idea of where they want to go.' Lenin.*

Help your coachee think about a goal or aim that motivates them. Some commentators use the concept of setting a personal vision – an objective that excites and enthuses them. Some people could strive to achieve a very aspirational and lofty goal. Others may seek only something that interests them and has some element of personal challenge involved. But if it's not something that a coachee has any particularly strong feelings about, it's probably not that worthwhile a goal – so why should they bother with it at all?

Appreciating different drivers

Different people are motivated in different ways. Research has identified three broad motivating forces or values in most people's working lives:

■ **Achievement.** Some people are driven by the need to perform better, win or prove themselves by beating the odds. They may enjoy working under pressure and can be motivated by the sheer thrill of accomplishing results.

- **Affiliation.** Others are driven by the need to establish and maintain close relationships with people that they respect or care for. They like to feel useful to other people – it might be colleagues or customers – and are motivated by being able to be part of a social group.

- **Power/status.** Still others look for the opportunity to have influence over others. They like to be highly regarded by others or have the authority to make others comply with their wishes.

What do you think might energise and engage your coachee?

Avoid imposing your values on a coachee. A goal has to be right for them, not you.

3. IDENTIFYING A LONG-TERM GOAL

Help your coachee to establish a suitably engaging goal with questions such as:

■ 'What would you like to achieve in your career?'

■ 'What would you realistically like to be doing in five years' time?'

■ 'Who do you admire that you have worked with? What is it that you admire about them? And would you want to be like them in any way?'

■ 'Thinking about what is going on in the organisation as well as the external market, what sort of development would you like in the coming months/year?'

■ 'What sorts of projects would you like to be involved with in the future?'

■ 'What would you like to get out of these coaching sessions?'

Further questions could include:

■ 'What skills do you need to make your job more enjoyable? How could you get those skills?'

■ 'What would you like to happen that is not happening at the moment?'

■ 'Which aspects of your job frustrate you or do you not enjoy? Are there any ways you could change your job to make it better?'

■ 'In which department or for which person would you like to be working?'

Make sure that you ask further questions to encourage coachees to elaborate in as much detail as possible on their goals. But goals also have to involve the emotions as much as the rational part of a coachee's brain in order to be really motivating. Challenge coachees to use their imagination – ask them how it would *feel* to achieve that goal or vision. You could ask questions such as:

■ 'What would it feel like if you achieved this goal? Project yourself into the future and describe what your career would be like if you achieve it.'

■ 'How disappointed would you be if you didn't achieve this goal?'

If a goal does not inspire, motivate or at least interest a coachee – try again.

Summarising the goal

Don't worry about trying to get a coachee to decide their goals in perfect detail. It is more important to help a coachee to establish a sense of direction for the future. However, you might find it useful to get the coachee to summarise their thoughts by completing a sentence such as:

- 'By the end of next year, I aim to have. . .'
- 'Within three years, I would like to be in a position to. . .'

This sentence can be as long or as short as the coachee likes. However, you need to make sure that this goal or vision is one that the coachee really wants. In fact, to be a really good source of motivation, the goal can be quite selfish. It doesn't matter if your coachee wants to earn more money to be able to buy a bigger car. Who cares if a coachee just wants a promotion to show off to family and friends? If the individual's long-term goal is not incompatible with the organisation's goals, selfishness can be a good thing.

Finally, make a note of the coachee's long-term goal, and refer back to it later on.

4. ESTABLISHING A STARTING POINT

Now let's figure out what skills and abilities will help your coachee reach his or her goal.

Good questions to start with could include some of the following:

- 'What's happening in your team at the moment? And how does it affect you?'

- 'What are you good at? What would you say your strengths are?'

- 'What do you think your weaknesses are? What do you need to improve?'

- 'What's stopping you at the moment from achieving what you want to do?'

Although these are good questions to start off a discussion, you will need to get into greater detail. For example, if a coachee talks about a particular aspect of the job that he or she likes or dislikes, you could use further questions to explore the situation such as:

- 'Why, in particular, do you dislike / like it?'
- 'How often does this happen?'
- 'When does this happen?'

Ask questions to help a coachee to identify the reality of their situation as opposed to what they choose to believe about themselves and their circumstances.

Domains of strength and weakness

When talking about strengths and weaknesses, there are many different domains of skill and knowledge that are required at work. The following list may help you to cover most of the skills that are important at work:

- **People skills** – e.g. communication and presentation skills as well as influence and persuasion. For coachees with teams of their own, this could also include managerial and leadership skills.

■ **Judgement and decision-making skills** – including the ability to analyse information, manipulate and calculate data, and make timely decisions.

■ **Functional areas of skill** – e.g. technical IT skills, knowledge of employment law, expertise in building financial models, understanding of markets or competitors, and so on.

■ **Personal attributes** – these include traits and qualities such as tenacity and integrity as well as good listening skills and the ability to understand what motivates other people.

Use these skill domains as a prompt for your own questions. As a coach, your role is to probe beneath the initial responses that the coachee provides you with. For example, a coachee might say, 'I don't know what I'm good at' – in which case you would have to challenge and help the coachee to identify areas of relative strength. Conversely, a coachee might argue that, 'I don't really have any weaknesses' – again, you would need to challenge this assertion as it is extremely unlikely that anyone is uniformly strong across all of the areas of skill and knowledge that are required to do a job effectively. Eventually, however, you will be able to build up a picture of what a coachee perceives to be their own strengths and weaknesses.

5. THINKING ABOUT IMPACT ON OTHERS

The previous section should help you to gain an idea of how the coachee perceives him or herself. However, the more important step in the coaching process is to help coachees to develop a greater awareness of how they are perceived *by others*. There are many occasions when an individual does something with a particular intention, but ends up communicating a completely different message to others.

The biggest barrier to success is often other people's perceptions of us.

Encourage your coachee to think about the many different people that they interact with:

- their boss

- colleagues within their team or department

- colleagues in the rest of the organisation

- those reporting directly to them or others who they are responsible for

- customers or clients.

You could use some of the following questions to prompt the coachee's thinking about how he or she is perceived by others:

- 'How do you think other people might describe you?'

- 'Do you agree with what you think they say about you?'

- 'Do you think they ever misunderstand your behaviour or intentions?'

- 'Do you have any abilities or talents that others don't think you have? What are they?'

IN SUMMARY

This third step in the five-stage model is to help coachees to define a realistic goal for the future and assess accurately their strengths and weaknesses. In doing so, be prepared to:

- Challenge any negative and overly positive beliefs that a coachee may have.

- Help your coachee choose a goal, objective or vision that excites them and is going to make them want to invest time and effort in working towards it.

- Get your coachee to start talking about their likes and dislikes, hopes and fears, perceived strengths and weaknesses.

- Help your coachee to gain a better understanding of how their intentions and behaviours might affect other people.

5 · Providing Feedback

'Coaching is about enhancing performance. So gather feedback on current performance to spur your coachee into action.'

In this Chapter:

Coaching is different from counselling. While counselling is aimed at making a person feel good about themselves, coaching is not. Coaching aims to develop others to become more committed and effective in their work.

However, it can be difficult to change a coachee's bad behaviour for the better if he or she does not see the need to change. As such, gathering feedback from colleagues or even customers provides better evidence that will persuade the coachee of the need to change.

Feedback is useful for pointing out shortcomings that need rectifying, but is just as important for highlighting good points for the coachee to build on too.

IS THIS YOU?

- I don't really want to give feedback. People don't seem to take notice of the comments that I have made in the past.

- My coachee has almost no awareness of how she is perceived by the other people in her team.

- My coachee keeps saying 'I can't change' and I don't know how to persuade her that she can.

■ I find it much easier to be positive about someone's strengths than to tell them what I honestly feel about their weaknesses.

■ I am worried that my coachee will just disregard the feedback. How can I help him to think about it and take it on board?

1. PREPARING TO GIVE FEEDBACK

It can be difficult for coachees to accept – let alone act on – what they don't want to hear. In order to make your case compelling, you need to prepare and choose your words carefully.

It is common for many of us to talk about 'strengths' and 'weaknesses'. However, the word 'weakness' is very emotive and implies that there is something wrong with a person – the *Oxford English Dictionary* defines one meaning of the word as 'a defect'. When giving feedback, it is therefore a good idea to refer to 'areas for improvement' or 'areas for development' instead of 'weaknesses' as these other terms suggest that action can be taken to improve or develop – whereas defective things tend to be discarded.

Tips for giving feedback

The following guidelines will help you to give feedback that is as painless and useful to the coachee as possible:

- **Be specific.** Saying 'your work is great' is less useful than telling a coachee that 'your colleagues liked the quality of the report you wrote'. Similarly, complaining about 'poor work' is less useful than saying exactly what was poor with the work.

- **Cite examples and evidence to back up your claims.** To support a claim that, for example, 'people think you are lazy', you should add an observation of behaviour that cannot be disputed such as 'you were late for work three times in the last month'.

- **Separate hearsay from fact.** For example, don't say, 'your presentation wasn't very good' if you actually mean, 'someone thought that your presentation wasn't very good'.

Giving feedback can be one of the trickiest and most uncomfortable tasks a coach has to do. You need to be accurate and honest – but at the same time motivating and never threatening.

2. CHOOSING RESPONDENTS

If you decide to gather feedback from other people, you will need to choose a number of 'respondents' to comment or respond on the coachee's performance at work.

Because you are coaching the individual, however, you need to work with your coachee to choose the respondents. Of course you can suggest respondents that you think would be suitable to give feedback, but you must listen if the coachee believes that another person would be more appropriate.

The more respondents you talk to, the richer will be your picture of how a coachee is perceived. However, gathering feedback is a time-consuming process. In practice then, you should aim to get feedback from at least four or six respondents who have had quite a lot of contact with the coachee. Less than four respondents may give you an unbalanced view, whereas many more would have diminishing returns.

Choose respondents who will give a candid 'warts and all' view of your coachee. Pleasantries and praise are of little use in assisting a coachee to develop.

Try to speak to a mix of colleagues at both more senior as well as more junior levels within the organisation. You might also wish to ask the opinions of a few customers or even suppliers. Having discussions with a wide range of respondents will allow you to see whether a coachee behaves equally to all people.

3. GATHERING FEEDBACK

The best way to collect feedback is to have a discussion with someone − preferably face to face. However, doing it over the telephone is fine when you don't have the time or if it is not geographically convenient.

Respondents need time to gather their thoughts and think of relevant examples, so give respondents advance notice − maybe a quick telephone call or a short letter explaining that you would like to speak to them. If you do not know the respondent well, you might have to explain who you are and that you are coaching a particular individual.

A step-by-step guide

When you actually come to having the discussion, collecting feedback in a logical fashion will ensure that you don't miss anything:

- **Re-introduce yourself.** Briefly explain the purpose and importance of collecting feedback.

- **Ask whether the respondent is happy to go 'on the record'.** Many people would rather not give negative feedback for fear of reprisal from coachees. Giving respondents the opportunity to be quoted anonymously may encourage them to be more honest. If a respondent would prefer not to be named, you should ensure that any comments they make are disguised so as not to give away their identity when you give the feedback to the coachee.

- **Start asking questions about strengths first.** Ask for specific examples and evidence of strengths. So if a respondent says, 'Her work was good', you should be asking

'What exactly was good about it?'

■ **Then ask about areas for improvement.** Again, to be useful to the coachee, rather than simply accepting that 'His presentations weren't very good', you could ask 'Why weren't they very good?'

■ **Finish by asking for suggestions as to how the coachee might improve.** When reporting these to the coachee, make sure that you mention that these were suggestions from respondents rather than from you.

At the end of each discussion, remember to thank the respondent for their time.

Collecting a complete picture

When you are talking to respondents, you may find that they struggle to come up with strengths or weaknesses. Although the following list is far from comprehensive, you could try prompting them in areas such as:

■ handling customers or clients

■ dealing with junior staff/peers/the coachee's boss

■ level of motivation, initiative and hard work

- time management, planning, organisation skills and attention to detail

- oral communication including presentation and public speaking skills

- computing, numeracy and writing skills

- ability to work under pressure and handle stress

- analytical and decision-making skills.

Once you have collected all of the feedback, you should collate a report – even if it is just some written notes for yourself. However, most coachees prefer to have a report that they can take away and think about, so consider typing up a few bullet points summarising their main strengths and areas for improvement. However, do remember if any respondents said they would prefer not to have their name attributed to specific comments.

If respondents see problems with your coachee – the onus is on you to encourage the coachee to change how they behave.

4. GIVING NEGATIVE FEEDBACK

The truth can be hard for some people to take. We have already discussed the topic of demonstrating empathy – and there are few occasions when it will be more important to be empathetic than when giving negative feedback.

If you sense that the negative feedback goes very much against what the coachee honestly believes about him or herself, you may need to handle the situation with additional sensitivity. Put yourself in their shoes and try to imagine how you would feel if you were going to be told what you are about to tell your coachee.

> *Give a coachee time to take in and reflect on negative feedback.*

5. GIVING POSITIVE FEEDBACK

Congratulating good performance is just as important as identifying where people are going wrong. Receiving only negative feedback can be very demoralising. A demoralised coachee will switch off and refuse to listen, or even decide not to take part in any more coaching to protect his or her feelings.

> *Everyone is good at something! Try to balance negative feedback with some positive feedback.*

But be careful not to overdo it by giving too much positive feedback. Receiving too much positive feedback is like eating too much of a good thing – you can easily lose your appetite for it very quickly. Also watch the tone of your voice – it can be easy to come across as patronising or insincere if you are not careful.

6. ELICITING REACTIONS TO FEEDBACK

Give your coachee time to absorb the feedback and think through its ramifications. You then need to give your coachee a chance to react to what the respondents have said. Suitable questions could include:

■ 'How do you feel about the feedback?'

■ 'Do you think the feedback is fair?'

■ 'Are there any comments that shocked or disappointed you? What are they?'

■ 'Are there any pleasant surprises in what people said about you? What are they?'

In a situation where the feedback is very critical of a coachee, he or she could react in a number of different ways. For example:

■ **Coachees can become defensive.** It is not uncommon to hear coachees using phrases such as 'it wasn't my fault because. . .' or 'I'm not the only person to do it – no one else in the department is any better'. The way to coach someone through negative feedback is to focus on why people might have a particular perception. You could ask 'Why do you think people raised it as an issue then?'

■ **Coachees can become angry.** A common response might be for people to respond that 'someone has an axe to grind' or 'they've got it in for me'. Some coachees might even go on the attack, criticising you (e.g. 'how can you sit there telling me this when you're just as bad?'). As a coach, your role may be to let your coachee get their feelings and anger out in the open. Once they have calmed down, they are much more likely to be able to talk rationally about how to move forwards and improve.

It can be easy for coachees to obsess over the exact words that are used to describe them. However, you should try to make coachees think about the underlying meaning of the comments rather than the exact words used.

Encourage a coachee to focus on the 'big picture' themes rather than the minutiae of the feedback.

IN SUMMARY

Feedback is a powerful tool for injecting a dose of reality into a coachee's assessment of their own performance and in setting realistic goals for their work and career. In this fourth step of the five-stage model, think about how you are going to use feedback to greatest effect:

- Help your coachee to choose respondents as opposed to picking respondents on behalf of your coachee.

- Use your skill to gather specific, useful feedback – both positive and negative – from respondents.

- Be sensitive and empathetic when giving negative feedback – no one finds it easy to hear bad things about themselves.

- Don't overdo positive feedback as too much good news loses its impact.

Then give the coachee an opportunity to take on board and react to the feedback before moving on to the next stage of generating options and planning how to change.

6 · Making Changes

'Setting goals is pointless unless you also put in place a plan of practical steps to act upon it.'

In this Chapter:

1 GENERATING IDEAS AND MAKING CHOICES

2 PROVIDING RESOURCES

3 AGREEING A PLAN

4 KEEPING THE MOMENTUM GOING

5 OFFERING ONGOING SUPPORT

6 SOLVING SPECIFIC PROBLEMS

In Chapter 4 we discussed helping a coachee to set an overall goal for their work or career. The next step in the five-stage model is to think about the actions that he or she could take to achieve that goal. It's time to decide how to change for the better.

However, your job doesn't end with sending a coachee away to work towards their goal. You have to be there to provide ongoing support – to tackle any obstacles that may arise as well as to offer encouragement and other resources – to ensure your coachee makes progress towards their goal.

IS THIS YOU?

■ My coachee has decided that his goal is to get promoted by next January, but how can we achieve it?

■ My coachee finds it a struggle to come up with ideas on how to tackle the issues that he faces.

■ How can I keep an eye on the progress that my coachees are making without appearing distrusting or seeming that I am checking up on them?

■ I need to find a way to be supportive but not directive in helping my coachees to reach their career goals.

■ My coachee is really struggling to make progress and I don't know how I can redirect her efforts.

1. GENERATING IDEAS AND MAKING CHOICES

Now that you have established what your coachee wants and how he or she is performing at the moment, you need to figure out what options are available for improving their performance. You need to invite suggestions and ideas from the coachee as to what actions he or she could take.

Generating ideas

Think of this step as a brainstorming session between yourself and a coachee. Useful questions to get the discussion going could include:

■ 'There are lots of things we could work on. What do you think some possible actions might be?'

■ 'Given the assessment we've done of your strengths and weaknesses, what steps do you think you need to take to achieve your career goals?'

■ 'What are you going to do to improve on your areas for development?'

■ 'How are you going to improve how other people see you?'

■ 'What alternatives might there be to that approach?'

■ 'When you have faced similar tricky situations, how have you dealt with them in the past?'

Focus initially on thinking creatively about actions – don't worry for the moment whether a particular idea is practicable or not.

Remember that your role is to help a coachee to come up with ideas rather than tell them what you think they should be doing. Even if a coachee seems to be overlooking some ideas or solutions that seem obvious to you, try to use questions to facilitate the coachee's thinking wherever possible. However, if you feel that a coachee is still missing a key point, first ask for the coachee's permission to contribute your thoughts – otherwise you risk telling rather than coaching. You could ask, 'Would you mind if I make a suggestion here?'

Finally, coaching is not just about working on areas for development. If a coachee has particular strengths, you should spend a little time making sure that the coachee understands the importance of also continuing to do what he or she is doing well.

Prioritising actions

Once you have generated a number of possible actions, you need to choose which ones to do. You can't expect a coachee to do everything at once. So the next step is to choose actions that will have the greatest impact with the least time and effort.

One way of doing this could be to examine how much time and effort would be required to get a benefit. Start by writing out a full list of possible actions on a blank sheet of paper. Then draw up a two-by-two cost versus benefit matrix as shown in Figure 1.

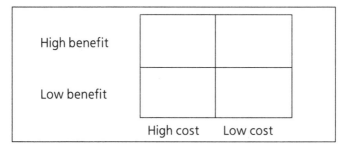

Figure 1. Cost versus benefit matrix

Take each of the ideas that the coachee has come up with and help your coachee to consider:

■ What would the costs (in terms of effort, energy, time, money) be of investing in an action? Would it take a lot of cost or relatively little?

■ What benefits would that action generate? Would the benefit of executing that idea be large or small?

Write each idea into the appropriate box on the matrix. And then prioritise the actions as follows:

■ The ones to focus on would be the ones in the top right-hand quadrant – the 'quick win' activities that should achieve the greatest benefits with the least effort, time or other cost.

■ Then identify the 'slow grow' areas – the actions in the top left-hand quadrant that could also make a big difference to the performance of your coachee, but may require more time and effort. These are the second most important actions to work on.

■ Don't worry about the rest of the list for the moment. Keep the list and refer back to it when you've worked on some of the 'quick wins' and 'slow grows' first.

Further prioritising

However, the matrix is only one way of prioritising actions. An alternative (or even additional) method might be to talk through each of the ideas:

■ 'Looking at these ideas, which do you find most appealing? Why?'

■ 'What are the risks or downsides of each option?'

■ 'What would you expect to gain by choosing any of these alternatives?'

■ 'How time consuming would each option be?'

■ 'How comfortable would you feel about pursuing these ideas?'

Also, keep in mind that **you are coaching, not teaching**. There are not always going to be right or wrong answers as to what the coachee should do. Your job is to help a coachee to commit to taking actions that they feel comfortable with.

> *Avoid spoon-feeding ideas to your coachee. Get your coachee to do the thinking.*

2. PROVIDING RESOURCES

Your role doesn't end when you have helped a coachee to produce a list of actions. It is now your job to help your coachee to achieve them. So think about the kinds of resources that a coachee could use:

■ **Colleagues.** In many situations, practical, hands-on experience is often the key to improving in a skill, so would anyone be able to spend time teaching your coachee a new skill? Could your coachee shadow someone and learn by observation or even be seconded to another department? Encourage coachees to get in touch with other experts and research their options so that they can take personal responsibility for their own development.

- **Group activities.** You could encourage coachees to volunteer for project teams, working parties or committees to acquire new knowledge or skills. Coachees might also spend time together sharing ideas and best-practice tips with each other. Perhaps peer coaching between your coachees or a coachee and another peer on specific issues might also be appropriate.

- **Training courses.** It may be that there are specific training needs that only a specialist may be able to help with. For example, a coachee may need language tuition or instructing in a technical matter that no one else has the time or skill to teach. But because you are coaching, encourage your coachees to do the research into what courses might be appropriate.

- **Books and materials.** Some people prefer to learn by reading at their own pace. Again, ask your coachees if they would like help in researching books or journal articles that they could learn from.

- **Time out.** Sometimes, a coachee may need a few hours away from the day-to-day pressures of their current role to learn or practise something. Even if you are not a coachee's direct boss, you could still ask the boss to give him or her some time off. If you explain what you have been trying to do, many bosses can be quite amenable.

> *Resist the temptation to tell a coachee to use particular resources. Feel free to suggest – but avoid being prescriptive if you can help it.*

3. AGREEING A PLAN

Once you and the coachee have together agreed on a manageable number of actions, it will help to flesh them out, starting with the 'quick wins'. People are more likely to follow through with actions when they are specific and measurable. For example, a coachee's action to 'focus more on my client relationships' is vague and open to a variety of interpretations. On the other hand, 'I will telephone each of my four key clients once a day and set up a monthly meeting with each one' is much more precise and therefore actionable.

> *The act of writing out an action plan has similar power to formal contracting – it helps to formalise and reinforce what the coachee must actually do.*

I would strongly suggest that you help your coachee to create a written action plan in order to agree some targets. All this involves is breaking down each action into a number of components. Each of the components (and questions to ask) is as follows:

■ **The action itself** – 'What exactly are you going to do?'

■ **The aim or purpose of the action** – 'Why do you want to do this? What do you think this action will accomplish? How will it help you towards achieving your overall career goal?'

■ **Resources** – 'Who else might be involved in helping you? What other resources might you draw upon to help you in achieving this action?'

■ **A timescale** – 'When are you going to start doing this? And when do you think you should aim to have completed this by?'

■ **A way of measuring success or failure** – 'What will it look like if you succeed in doing this? Or what will the effect be if you are successful in achieving this?'

Sample action plan format

Many organisations encourage the use of an action plan format such as shown in Figure 2.

Action	Aim/purpose	Resources	Timescale	Measures

Figure 2. Action plan format

Feel free to adapt the format of Figure 2. Then, perhaps type it up or simply ask a coachee to write it out by hand. But the important part is to encourage your coachee to draw up a written action plan so that you can refer to it in later coaching sessions to measure progress.

4. KEEPING THE MOMENTUM GOING

Your first few sessions with new coachees should focus on getting to know about their interests and skills and then the areas of their working life that they would like to change. By the end of these initial sessions, you should aim to have worked up a draft action plan with a coachee.

Over the course of subsequent coaching sessions, however, your focus should quickly shift from **what** coachees want to achieve to **how** they are going to achieve it. As the weeks and months pass, your role increasingly becomes one of ensuring progress is being made against their plan.

At the outset of each new session, encourage your coachee to talk about the actions that they took and the results that they achieved. Try to discuss how things went and use questions to draw out the learning points from what they have tried and perhaps failed at or succeeded with. To make better use of the limited time in coaching sessions, you might wish to call coachees or send them an e-mail with a few questions to prepare their thoughts ahead of time.

Questioning to check progress

The following are useful questions for starting off a meeting:

- 'What would you like to talk about in this session? How can we make the best use of this time that we have available?'

- 'How is life treating you? How are things going generally?'

Then move on to questions about the action plan:

- 'How are you getting on with your action plan? How happy are you with your progress so far?'

- 'What seems to be working for you so far?'

- 'Is it taking you more or less time that you expected to. . .?'

- 'How easy are you finding it to. . .?'

- 'How did you get on the other day with. . .?'

Then continue to probe further. Ask about specific actions on the plan and their progress against it:

- 'What went well? What went badly?'

- 'Why did it go well or badly? Were you surprised that it did (or did not) work out that way?'

■ 'Are there any patterns to what has worked or failed so far?'

If the actions in the first draft of the action plan that you agreed upon are proving too difficult to achieve, you and your coachee may decide to scale them back a little. On the other hand, if things are going well and your coachee is making good progress, you may wish to set a more challenging goal or see what other actions your coachee could also be taking.

> **Work to provide the right level of challenge for your coachee. Too much challenge could seem overly daunting while too little could make it appear facile and unworthy of effort.**

Learning from mistakes

No one is perfect. We all make mistakes. But the key in coaching is to help coachees to learn from those mistakes, not to judge them.

Work with your coachee to identify the learning points from any mistakes:

- 'Why do you think it didn't turn out as you expected?'

- 'Tell me exactly what you did.'

- 'What do you think we can learn from what happened?'

- 'What would you do if that particular situation cropped up again?'

It is particularly important, however, to ensure that your tone and manner do not in any way make coachees feel guilty or stupid. If they think that you are talking down to them, they will most likely refuse to talk openly about the mistake and try to cover it up instead.

Ensure that you adopt a neutral tone and manner when discussing mistakes.

5. OFFERING ONGOING SUPPORT

Coaching should include not only scheduled sessions but also support outside of them. Think about how you could provide advice and encouragement between sessions as well.

Consider, for example:

■ **Offering encouragement before particularly difficult tasks.** You should make efforts to be aware of when your coachee is about to embark on a task or event about which they are very anxious. You might want to wish them good luck – perhaps by dropping round to their desk with a few words of encouragement or even just by picking up the telephone or sending them a quick email.

■ **Acting as a coachee's conscience.** Some coachees can be more forgetful than others. If you think that any coachees might be in danger of letting their priorities slip, you might want to remind them of the commitments they have made. At times, this could be as simple as passing a coachee in the corridor and asking, 'How's it going?'.

■ **Giving timely feedback.** If you observe an instance of inappropriate behaviour, you may not want to risk waiting until the next session when the coachee might have forgotten about the incident. There may sometimes be greater value in taking a coachee aside and giving them the feedback there and then.

■ **Letting a coachee know that you are there.** If a coachee is struggling to tackle their work or the actions on their plan, you should make it clear to them that you are there to offer support whenever they need it. 'My door is always open' is a bit of a cliché, but can be very comforting if you say it and mean it.

Overcoming common obstacles

Your support is vital because there are many common obstacles that could derail your coachee's progress. Look out for:

■ **Laziness or a lack of motivation.** Some people may be apathetic or reluctant to develop themselves because they cannot see the benefit of change. It may be that the long-term goal that you helped a coachee to identify was not sufficiently exciting. Or perhaps it was genuinely engaging at the time, but the coachee's circumstances have changed. So how might you help the coachee to identify a new career goal that will get them inspired again?

- **An overly challenging action plan.** The long-term goal may be engaging and motivating. But perhaps the activities on their action plan seem too daunting or difficult to take on. If this is the case, how could you help them to rethink their action plan?

- **Overwork and tiredness.** Most people's workload varies. We all suffer peaks when we work long hours and never seem to get everything done. If a coachee is very overworked – perhaps because it is a historically busy time of the year or maybe because a colleague is on sick leave – it may be a good idea to let the coachee deal with the work crises at hand before asking them to focus on their action plan again.

- **Lack of confidence.** In such a case, the coachee may have the skills to do the job, but doubt their own ability to do so. Try to help your coachee to find small ways of practising the skill in order to boost their confidence. A coachee who is nervous about giving a presentation to a large group could perhaps do a dummy run with a small group of peers or even to you alone.

A coachee who is worried about disciplining a member of their team might find value in role playing the situation with you. Providing such opportunities will create a virtuous circle in which their increasing confidence allows them to become more and more adept at exercising the new skill.

■ **Lack of commitment or support from other people.** It is too often the case that other people can let us down. Perhaps a manager who offered to show your coachee how to operate a new system has been too busy to do so. Maybe a secondment into another team has failed to materialise. Or possibly a lack of funding has meant that a vital training course has had to be cancelled. Whatever the cause, you will have to work with your coachee to think of some other creative way to achieve a similar result.

Be aware of potential problems and think ahead to what you and your coachee could do in anticipation of them.

6. SOLVING SPECIFIC PROBLEMS

Numerous other problems will almost certainly crop up and threaten to undermine your coachee's progress. Personal development is never an easy task – and even a relatively small upset or setback could be enough for a coachee to want to give up entirely on their plan.

A coachee might be struggling to grasp the basic tenets of cost accounting. Or a coachee might have failed several times to persuade the marketing director about a new idea. Whatever the problem, your job is to help to resolve it. But remember that problems and failure can be very disheartening. So be prepared to be sensitive and empathetic if your coachee is agitated or worried.

Only when your coachee is calm enough should you try to discuss how best to resolve the situation. Remember, though, to open the discussion with questions as opposed to assertions:

■ 'What exactly have you tried so far? And why do you think it hasn't worked so far?'

- 'What other alternatives do you have? Don't worry whether they are realistic at this stage – let's discuss each of them in turn.'

- 'What else might we try?'

- 'What do you think the underlying problem is? And how are we going to tackle this problem?'

- 'Who else could you talk to for a different perspective?'

- 'Could anyone else help you with this? And how might you enlist their support?'

- 'Would you like to leave the problem for now, reflect on it and come back to it either later on today or in a later session?'

Again, focus on asking shrewd questions to help your coachee to find their own solutions. Only if all else fails, should you ask if there might be anything that you could do – for example to offer your opinion on the situation or perhaps to influence someone on your coachee's behalf.

Your role as a coach is not merely to sympathise with a coachee's problems but to challenge and push them to identify possible solutions. Don't confuse coaching with being a friend.

IN SUMMARY

Much of the coaching relationship should focus on the final stage of the five-stage model – checking a coachee's progress and ensuring that they stay on track. Try to:

■ Decide what actions would have the greatest positive impact on performance with the least energy or wasted time – a coachee can only undertake to make a few changes at a time.

■ Support your coachee by providing not only encouragement and advice but also help in finding other resources.

■ Work together to solve any problems that could derail a coachee's progress – all the while remembering to coach and not tell.

7 · Finishing on a High Note

'A good coach knows when it is time to end the coaching relationship.'

In this Chapter:

1 CELEBRATING SUCCESS

2 CONCLUDING THE COACHING
RELATIONSHIP

3 REVIEWING YOUR COACHING
PERFORMANCE

4 AVOIDING COMMON PITFALLS

5 COACHING ON A DAY-TO-DAY BASIS

6 DEVELOPING YOURSELF

The five-stage model set out in the previous chapters
provides a solid framework for you to be able to coach effec-

tively. However, becoming a great coach requires experience and some self-analysis. Experience will come with time. But you must make a dedicated effort to appraise your own performance as a coach and think about how you could improve.

Whether you have been coaching for a few months or many years, you should be careful not to think that you've 'made it'. There is a fine line between confidence and arrogance – and the arrogant coach is of little use to anyone. So apply the principles of coaching to yourself – keep reviewing your performance and developing yourself. And if you are coaching people and getting feedback on them, shouldn't you also have a coach and have feedback collected on you?

Coaching is not a skill to be used some of the time but not at others – it's a way of managing all of your relationships at work.

IS THIS YOU?

- I think that I am a reasonably good coach but how can I get better?

- I'm not sure if I am actually coaching or still merely instructing, teaching or delegating work.

- I feel that my coachee and I should be making progress faster than we are.

- I am part of a team that should be achieving much more than we do – but I don't know whether it would be appropriate for me to coach it along.

- I'm happy to coach others but don't have the time for some-one to coach me.

1. CELEBRATING SUCCESS

Celebrating success helps coachees to realise that they can reach the goals that they set for themselves, which should spur them onto greater efforts in the future. It promotes a virtuous circle of effort and reward, which forms a key part of the ongoing process of coaching.

People find it hugely motivating to receive recognition for their work. However, I would make a difference between praise and rewards:

- **Praise good efforts.** If someone puts a lot of time and effort into a task or project, they deserve acknowledgement for it – even if they did not necessarily get the results that were hoped for. Unmitigated praise is a powerful tool for creating good feelings and reinforcing performance. However, be careful not to overdo it as a coach who says 'great work, well done' only occasionally for truly good work is much more believable than one who says it all of the time.

- **Reward good results.** When someone has worked hard **and** achieved the desired outcome for a significant task or project, it may be appropriate to offer a reward that is more tangible than praise alone. However, do consider whether you should be offering rewards at all. For example, if you are not a coachee's line manager – what would their current line manager think? Should the achievement of a goal be reward enough in itself? Could the reward inadvertently be seen to be patronising?

Praise good efforts, and reward good results.

When rewarding one coachee, however, be careful to make it clear to all of your coachees as well as others in the team exactly why the rewards were given out. The last thing that you want is for the people around you to perceive that you have favourites.

Using rewards creatively

Also think about all of the forms that rewards can take – they can be both financial as well as non-financial. Think about giving someone the afternoon off for completing a project. Or hire a sports car for the weekend for a top performer.

But the sort of reward that you might offer depends entirely on the circumstances as well as the person that you are rewarding. For example, offering a £20 gift voucher may be appropriate for a data entry clerk for a week of exceptional performance. On the other hand, a senior manager might reasonably expect a £20,000 pay rise for meeting the year's performance targets.

2. CONCLUDING THE COACHING RELATIONSHIP

If you are coaching an individual for a specific issue – perhaps helping a remedial coachee to fill a development need or supporting a high potential coachee in finding a more challenging role within the organisation – then there will come a time when you will need to end the relationship.

One way to bring the relationship to a satisfactory end might be to repeat the feedback exercise detailed in Chapter 5. If you wrote a report when you first gathered feedback, it should be easy for you to compare how a coachee is currently doing with how they performed in the past. Hopefully, at this stage, both you and the respondents will have seen some positive changes in the coachee's behaviour that will be worth celebrating.

In your final coaching session, you should also review the entire coaching relationship:

■ 'What are the key lessons that you have learnt over the past weeks/months?'

- 'What have you done that went particularly well? What were you most pleased with?'

- 'What went badly or less well? Why did it go wrong? What would you do differently if you faced the same situation again?'

- 'How do you think you have changed in these weeks/months? What other areas do you think you still need to work on over the coming weeks/months?'

- 'Now that you have achieved some of your goals, what else might you set as a goal for the future?'

Finally, ask for some candid feedback on your performance as a coach. However, make it clear to your coachee that you are not simply looking for plaudits. You would value your coachee's opinion about not only what was good, but also what could be better. Try questions such as:

- 'What did you find most useful about having a coach?'

- 'What could I have done differently as a coach?'

- 'If you could give me one piece of advice that would improve my coaching skills, what would it be?'

3. REVIEWING YOUR COACHING PERFORMANCE

In order to be a good coach, you need to keep asking yourself: Are you doing as good a job as you possibly can?

After every single session that you have with a coachee, take just a few minutes to consider the following:

■ Did you make progress over the course of the session? Specifically what was it that you did that helped the coachee to progress?

■ What did the coachee get out of the session?

■ In retrospect, was there anything that you **should** have done during the session? If there was, don't worry – do it next time, but in the meantime learn from your experience.

■ What lessons can you take away to apply with other coachees?

Review your performance to revitalise and renew your coaching sessions.

4. AVOIDING COMMON PITFALLS

Some people find coaching extraordinarily difficult because it requires them to think and act in a way that feels alien to them. Others find it very straightforward. However, most people – even the most experienced of coaches – can make mistakes occasionally.

Teaching, not coaching

Effective coaching requires a careful balance between asking good questions and knowing when to give direct feedback or constructive criticism. Probably the single most common trap is for coaches to resort to teaching rather than coaching. You might be talking at your coachee rather than talking with him or her if you can answer yes to one or more of the following:

■ Do you find yourself talking for more than about half of each session?

■ Do you ever find yourself interrupting your coachee to say something more important?

■ Do you set the agenda for each meeting? (You should be allowing the coachee to lead the pace at which you work together.)

■ Do you often find yourself using phrases such as 'you're wrong' or 'I think you should. . .'?

If you do find yourself teaching rather than coaching, you might want to review the sections on questioning and listening in Chapter 3. Explain to your coachee that you might have been doing too much of the talking and encourage your coachee to tell you when he or she thinks you have been talking too much.

> *Focus on 'pulling' a coachee towards their goal rather than 'pushing' them towards it.*

Moving at the wrong pace

Another common trap is to move the discussion on either too quickly or too slowly for a coachee. You can see how this could be a problem for a teacher who has to cope with a class of students of mixed abilities. But, in a one-to-one situation, you should never make this mistake.

For instance, you may think that a particular coachee is very intelligent and want her to plan actions as quickly as possible – but she may value most spending time on choosing the right long-term goal before moving on. The opposite could also happen too – that you are moving too slowly and inadvertently patronising a coachee.

Again, questions provide part of the solution here. Try asking:

- 'Are we moving at the right pace? Should we speed up or slow down?'

- 'Would you feel comfortable if we moved on to the next topic now?'

- 'What do you most value from these coaching sessions? What is it that I do or could be doing that is of the most help to you?'

But use your eyes as well as your ears. Does your coachee appear frustrated by the lack of pace? Or do they seem anxious or confused by moving too fast?

Becoming frustrated by a lack of progress

It can be easy to become frustrated with a coachee when you can see no visible signs of progress. In such a situation, you should:

- **Review whether your coachee's long-term goal is still appropriate.** Is the goal too difficult? Have circumstances perhaps changed since you set it? If the goal is no longer appropriate, you may need to set a new long-term goal together.

- **Re-assess the coachee's action plan.** Are these actions still appropriate and achievable? If not, what actions might be better suited for your coachee? Or, if the actions are still appropriate, then consider the obstacles or specific problems that might be preventing your coachee from making further progress.

- **Ask yourself whether you are offering enough resources and support outside of coaching sessions.** Are you keeping tabs on your coachee's performance on a regular basis outside of your coaching sessions? Have you done enough to build a strong rapport and relationship with your coachee?

■ **Above all, avoid showing any frustration or irritation at the lack of progress.** Showing any impatience could undermine the entire coaching process.

5. COACHING ON A DAY-TO-DAY BASIS

The skills of coaching are helpful for dealing with many people on a day-to-day basis at work – whether it is your peers, your boss or perhaps even customers and suppliers that you wish to influence. Why not use your newfound coaching skills to your advantage with these people too?

Even if you are not in a formal coaching relationship, think about occasions when you could use the skills involved in coaching. For example, you might be in a situation where you could:

■ Ask insightful and probing questions to understand more accurately the needs of a customer or colleague.

■ Listen to and be empathetic with a team member who is distressed about a personal problem.

■ Give feedback to a colleague on some aspect of their performance that concerns you.

If giving feedback to colleagues, praise publicly but criticise privately.

Coaching upwards

Your boss and other senior individuals may at times benefit from your guidance, but you must apply your skills in a more subtle fashion because it's highly unlikely that they would agree to being formally coached by you. However, you can still offer useful feedback and challenge their thinking following the principles we have already discussed. In addition to the usual guidelines, however, try to:

■ **Choose an appropriate moment.** If you embarrass a senior person in front of the people who work for them, you will almost certainly regret it later. Choose a moment when your boss is in a reasonable mood and the two of you are alone.

■ **Start by asking for feedback on your performance.** For example, if you had both just come out of a tricky meeting with a client, you might ask whether there was anything that you could have done better.

■ **Then ask for permission to give your boss feedback.** For example, 'would you mind if I gave you a small piece of feedback on something that I observed in that meeting just now?'. If your boss declines the feedback, save it for another, perhaps better, occasion.

Coaching a team

You can also use your coaching skills to help any team or group of people become more effective in how they interact with each other too. However, you do not have to announce that you are going to coach the group or try to wrest control of the team from its established leader.

Think of group meetings as an abbreviated coaching relationship. Consider the following guidelines to help meetings run more smoothly:

■ **Help the group to establish its goals.** What does it hope to achieve — either by the end of each meeting or the end of the project?

■ **Brainstorm possible ideas.** What ideas does the group have for how it could achieve its goals? Try to get every person in the group to contribute. Look out for the quieter individuals and try to draw them into the discussion as well.

■ **Prioritise ideas.** Perhaps you could use the two-by-two matrix or questioning techniques covered in Chapter 6 to help the group identify the best ways forwards.

■ **Turn ideas into concrete actions.** Use questions to encourage the group to think about actions they could take and a plan that they could follow.

Leading a team is an entire topic in its own right, but these simple guidelines should help a group to work together more effectively.

6. DEVELOPING YOURSELF

Good coaches are role models for the power of coaching. An

individual who tries to coach others but is not open to being coached will suffer from a lack of credibility. We can all think of examples of people who say, 'do as I **say**, not as I **do**' – and the bottom line is that we rarely have much respect for them.

So try to live by the principles of coaching yourself. Begin by identifying a long-term goal for your own career. What motivates and interest you? What do you hope to achieve in your future career? Then ask yourself:

■ What actions could I take to achieve my goal?

■ What obstacles am I likely to have to overcome?

Secondly, find a coach for yourself. Seek out an individual who has the qualities outlined in Chapter 1. If such a person does not exist within your own organisation, could you seek a coach or mentor outside of the organisation? When you have identified the right coach, prepare to be open-minded and listen to what he or she has to say.

You should also obtain feedback from the people you work with in order to identify further areas for development. The following tips may encourage people to be more candid with you:

■ Explain that you are seeking feedback purely for the purpose of self-development.

■ Show your respect for what each person has to say. Whether you agree with what is being said or not, the individual has reasons and a right to feel the way that they do.

■ If you don't agree with feedback, do question it – but make sure that you avoid behaving defensively.

■ Show your appreciation and thank people for giving you feedback.

■ Make sure that you act upon any feedback and make an effort to demonstrate to whoever gave you the feedback that you tried to act upon it.

Practise what you preach. If you don't have a coach, can you honestly expect your coachees to respect you?

You should also aim to keep abreast of coaching resources and new coaching techniques to incorporate into your method of coaching. Look for opportunities to network with other coaches and learn from each other. Borrow a book from a library or get your organisation to invest in a copy of any new manuals on coaching and people development. Check magazines and journals for articles on coaching. Search the Internet for resources too. Keep learning.

IN SUMMARY

Coaching is a dynamic skill — you need to invest time and effort to keep your coaching methods up to scratch. In particular:

■ Keep assessing your skills as a coach. Ask yourself after every single coaching session: what could I have done even better?

■ Be careful not to fall into the trap of teaching rather than coaching.

■ Find a person that you trust to coach you. If coaching is good enough for others, then it must be good enough for you too.

■ Keep learning and growing as a coach. Search for opportunities to learn from fellow coaches, books and other resources.

All in all, coaching is a vital skill for success at work. Apart from entering into formal coaching relationships, you could also use your skill to develop your boss as well as any teams or groups that you may work with.

Good luck.